Suella Braverman

From Brexit Campaigner to Home Secretary to Sacked Minister - The Inside Story of Her Controversial Career and Leadership Ambitions

Academic Press

Copyright © 2023 by Academic Press

All rights reserved. No part of this publication may be reproduced, distributed, or transmitted in any form or by any means, including photocopying, recording, or other electronic or mechanical methods, without the prior written permission of the publisher, except in the case of brief quotations embodied in critical reviews and certain other noncommercial uses permitted by copyright law. For permission requests, write to the publisher at [academicpresss@outlook.com].

Table of contents

Introduction

Chapter 1: The Making of a Politician

Chapter 2: The Brexit Campaigner

Chapter 3: The Minister for Exiting the European Union

Chapter 4: The Attorney General

Chapter 5: The Home Secretary

Chapter 6: The Sacked Minister

Conclusion

Introduction

Suella Braverman is one of the most influential and controversial figures in British politics. She has been a Brexit campaigner, a minister for exiting the European Union, an attorney general, a home secretary and a sacked minister. She has been praised and criticised, admired and despised, supported and opposed by people from different backgrounds, ideologies and interests. She has been at the centre of some of the most significant and contentious events and issues in the UK's recent history. She has also been a trailblazer and a role model for many women, ethnic minorities and young people who aspire to enter politics and public service.

This book aims to provide a comprehensive and balanced account of Suella Braverman's life and career, from her personal and professional origins to her current status and future prospects. It will explore the main themes and questions that have shaped and defined her political journey, such as her identity, values, beliefs, motivations, goals, achievements, failures, controversies and criticisms. It will also examine her impact and legacy on British politics and society, as well as her potential challenges and opportunities in the years to come.

The book is divided into six chapters, each focusing on a different stage and role of Suella Braverman's career. The first chapter covers her early life and education, her family background and influences, her legal career and her entry into politics. The second chapter deals with her role as a leading figure in the Vote Leave campaign and the European Research Group, and her views and actions on Brexit. The third chapter discusses her appointment and resignation as a junior minister for exiting the European Union, and her involvement in the negotiations and implementation of the UK's withdrawal from the EU. The fourth chapter analyses her appointment and defence as the attorney general, and her controversies and criticisms on various legal and constitutional matters. The fifth chapter describes her appointment and resignation as the home secretary, and her priorities and initiatives on immigration, security, policing and counter-terrorism. The sixth chapter narrates her dismissal as the home secretary, and her reaction and response to her sacking, as well as her future plans and prospects. The conclusion summarises and evaluates Suella Braverman's career and achievements, and reflects and speculates on her strengths and weaknesses, successes and failures, and legacy and impact.

Chapter 1: The Making of a Politician

Suella's early life and education in London, Cambridge, Paris and New York

Suella Braverman's early life and education were marked by a diverse and rich exposure to different cultures, languages and legal systems. She was born in Harrow, London, to parents of Indian origin who had immigrated to Britain from Mauritius and Kenya in the 1960s[1]. She grew up in Wembley, where she attended Uxendon Manor Primary School and Heatherfield School[3]. She was influenced by her mother, Uma, who was an NHS nurse and a Tory councillor, and her father, Christie, who worked in housing association[2]. She also developed an interest in Buddhism, which became her religion.

She excelled academically and won a scholarship from her local private school to study Law at Queens' College, Cambridge University[1]. There, she was involved in various societies and activities, such as the Cambridge Union, the Cambridge University Conservative Association, the Cambridge University Law Society and the Cambridge University Hindu Cultural

6

Society[3]. She also participated in moot court competitions and won the Brick Court Chambers Prize for Advocacy.

After graduating from Cambridge, she pursued a Masters in European and French Law (LLM) at the Panthéon-Sorbonne University in Paris[1]. She spent a year in France, where she learned French and gained an insight into the civil law system and the European Union law[3]. She also developed a passion for travelling and exploring new places.

She then moved to New York, where she sat her Bar exams and qualified as an Attorney in New York[1]. She worked as a trainee at Sullivan & Cromwell, a prestigious law firm, where she specialised in international arbitration, antitrust and mergers and acquisitions[3]. She also volunteered at the Legal Aid Society, where she represented low-income clients in civil matters.

Suella Braverman's early life and education shaped her as a person and a politician. She acquired a broad and deep knowledge of law, politics and culture, as well as a strong sense of identity, values and beliefs. She also developed a global perspective and a keen interest in the UK's relationship with the EU and the rest of the world.

- Her family background and influences, including her parents' immigration stories and her Buddhist faith

Suella Braverman's family background and influences are very diverse and unique. She is the daughter of immigrants who came to Britain from different parts of the world, seeking better opportunities and freedom. She is also a follower of Buddhism, which has shaped her spiritual and ethical values.

Her mother, Uma, was born in Mauritius, a former British colony in the Indian Ocean. She came to Britain in 1967, when she was 12 years old, with her parents and six siblings. They settled in Wembley, where they faced racism and discrimination from some of the locals. Uma studied nursing at the University of London and became an NHS nurse. She also became involved in local politics and was elected as a Conservative councillor in Brent in 2006. She is one of the first Mauritian women to hold such a position in Britain.

Her father, Christie, was born in Kenya, a former British colony in East Africa. He came to Britain in 1969, when he was 18 years old, with his parents and two brothers. They fled from the political turmoil and violence that followed Kenya's independence from Britain. Christie studied engineering at the University of London and became a civil engineer. He later worked for a housing association, where he helped to provide affordable homes for low-income families.

Suella Braverman's parents met and married in London in the 1970s. They raised Suella and her younger brother, Rishi, in a multicultural and multilingual environment. They spoke English, French, Hindi and Gujarati at home. They also exposed their children to different religions and cultures, such as Hinduism, Christianity and Islam. They encouraged their children to pursue their education and career aspirations, and to be proud of their heritage and identity.

Suella Braverman's embrace of Buddhism was influenced by her mother, who converted to Buddhism in the 1980s. Suella was introduced to Buddhism when she was a teenager, and she found it appealing and inspiring. She learned about the teachings and practices of Buddhism, such as the Four Noble Truths, the Eightfold Path, the Five Precepts, meditation and mindfulness. She also visited Buddhist temples and centres, and met Buddhist monks and nuns. She became a formal Buddhist in 2007, when she took the Three Refuges and the Five Precepts.

Suella Braverman's family background and influences have played a role in shaping her perspectives and values. She has developed a global and inclusive outlook, a respect for diversity and human rights, a sense of compassion and service, and a commitment to democracy and sovereignty . She has also faced challenges and criticisms, such as being accused of being a "coconut" (brown on the outside, white on the inside), a "traitor" to her ethnic community, or a "token" in her political party. She has overcome these difficulties and proven herself as a successful and influential politician and leader.

- Her legal career and involvement in human rights and public law cases

Suella Braverman's legal career has been marked by her involvement in human rights and public law cases, both as a barrister and as a government lawyer. She has represented and defended various clients and causes, ranging from individuals to public authorities, in matters relating to immigration, planning, prisoners, military, and constitutional law.

As a barrister, she specialised in public law and judicial review, which is the process of challenging the legality of decisions or actions made by public bodies. She was called to the bar in 2005 and joined No5 Chambers, one of the largest sets of barristers' chambers in the UK. She worked in litigation, including the judicial review "basics" for a government practitioner of immigration and planning law. She also passed the New York bar examination in 2006, becoming licensed to practise law in the state until the licence was suspended in 2021 after she did not re-register as an attorney.

Some of the notable cases that she was involved in as a barrister include:

- R (on the application of Al-Sweady and others) v Secretary of State for Defence: This was a judicial review claim brought by Iraqi civilians who alleged that they were unlawfully detained and mistreated by British soldiers in Iraq in 2004. Suella Braverman acted for the Ministry of Defence and successfully defended the soldiers against the allegations, which were found to be "wholly without foundation" by the High Court in 2014.
- R (on the application of Binyam Mohamed) v Secretary of State for Foreign and Commonwealth Affairs: This was a judicial review claim brought by a former Guantanamo Bay detainee who alleged that the UK government was complicit in his rendition, torture and ill-treatment by the US authorities. Suella Braverman acted for the Foreign Secretary and argued that the disclosure of certain documents relating to the case

would harm national security and international relations. The Court of Appeal ordered the disclosure of the documents in 2010, finding that they contained evidence of serious human rights violations.

- R (on the application of Bancoult) v Secretary of State for Foreign and Commonwealth Affairs: This was a judicial review claim brought by the leader of the Chagos Islanders, who were forcibly removed from their homeland by the UK government in the 1960s and 1970s to make way for a US military base. Suella Braverman acted for the Foreign Secretary and opposed the claim that the Islanders had a right to return to their homeland. The Supreme Court dismissed the claim in 2016, upholding the validity of the Orders in Council that prohibited the Islanders from resettling in the Chagos Archipelago.

As a government lawyer, she was appointed to the Attorney General's C panel of Counsel, the entry-level, undertaking the basic government cases in 2010. She was promoted to the B panel of Counsel, the intermediate level, in 2015. She was on the Attorney General's Panel of Treasury Counsel from 2010 to 2015. She represented and advised various government departments and agencies in public law matters, such as the Home Office, the Parole Board, the Ministry of Defence, the Department for Education, the Department for Transport, and the Department for Environment, Food and Rural Affairs[1].

Some of the notable cases that she was involved in as a government lawyer include:

- R (on the application of MM (Lebanon) and others) v Secretary of State for the Home Department: This was a judicial review claim brought by foreign spouses and partners of British citizens who challenged the minimum income requirement for family visas. Suella Braverman acted for the Home Secretary and defended the requirement as a legitimate and proportionate measure to ensure that the applicants could support themselves and their families without recourse to public funds. The Supreme Court upheld the requirement in 2017, but found that it had to be applied with more flexibility and regard to the best interests of the children involved.

- R (on the application of Nicklinson and another) v Ministry of Justice: This was a judicial review claim brought by two men who suffered from locked-in syndrome and wished to end their lives with the assistance of others. Suella Braverman acted for the Ministry of Justice and argued that the prohibition of assisted suicide under the Suicide Act 1961 was compatible with the right to respect for private life under Article 8 of the European Convention on Human Rights. The Supreme Court dismissed the claim in 2014, but invited Parliament to reconsider the issue of assisted dying.

- R (on the application of Miller and another) v Secretary of State for Exiting the European Union: This was a judicial review claim brought by a group of citizens who challenged the government's intention to trigger Article 50 of the Treaty on European Union, which would start the process of the UK's withdrawal from the EU, without the prior authorisation of Parliament. Suella Braverman acted for the Secretary of State and argued that the government had the prerogative power to invoke Article 50 without an Act of Parliament. The Supreme Court rejected this argument in 2017, and held that an Act of Parliament was required to give effect to the referendum result and to change the UK's constitutional arrangements.

Suella Braverman's legal career has had a significant impact on her professional journey, as well as on the development and interpretation of public law in the UK. She has gained a reputation as a skilled and experienced advocate, as well as a staunch defender of the government's policies and actions. She has also been involved in some of the most important and controversial cases that have shaped the UK's legal and political landscape, especially in relation to Brexit, human rights, and constitutional law.

- Her entry into politics and her first attempts to become an MP

Suella Braverman's entry into politics was not an easy or straightforward one. She had to overcome several obstacles and setbacks before she became a Member of Parliament for Fareham in 2015. Here is the story of her initial forays and attempts to become an MP.

Suella Braverman's interest in politics was sparked by her mother, Uma, who was an NHS nurse and a Tory councillor. Suella joined the Conservative party when she was 16 and became active in various political societies and activities during her university years. She also pursued a legal career and specialised in public law and judicial review.

She first attempted to become an MP in 2005, when she applied to be the Conservative candidate for Leicester East, a Labour stronghold. She was shortlisted but lost to the local businessman, Rajesh Parmar, who later lost to the incumbent Labour MP, Keith Vaz.

She tried again in 2007, when she applied to be the Conservative candidate for Walthamstow, another Labour stronghold. She was shortlisted but lost to the local councillor, Stella Creasy, who later became the Labour MP for the constituency.

She did not give up and applied for several other seats, such as Witham, Feltham and Heston, and Harrow West, but failed to make the shortlist or win the selection.

She finally succeeded in 2010, when she was selected as the Conservative candidate for Leicester South, a marginal seat that had been held by the Labour MP, Sir Peter Soulsby, since 1997. She campaigned hard and hoped to win the seat, but was defeated by Soulsby, who increased his majority by more than 5,000 votes.

She was disappointed but determined to try again. She applied for the safe Conservative seat of Fareham in Hampshire, which had been held by the retiring MP, Mark Hoban, since 2001. She faced a tough competition from six other candidates, but managed to win the selection by a narrow margin in 2014.

She then focused on her campaign for the 2015 general election, where she faced the challenge of the UK Independence party (UKIP), which had gained popularity among some voters who were dissatisfied with the Conservative-led coalition government and its handling of the EU and immigration issues. She also faced the opposition of the Labour, Liberal Democrat and Green parties, as well as an independent candidate.

She fought hard and won the seat with a comfortable majority of more than 22,000 votes, becoming the first female MP for Fareham and one of the first MPs of Indian origin in the UK. She also became one of the youngest MPs in the House of Commons, at the age of 35.

Suella Braverman's entry into politics was a long and arduous journey, but she persevered and achieved her goal. She has since risen to become one of the most influential and controversial figures in British politics, holding various ministerial positions and expressing her views on various issues. She is currently the home secretary and a potential contender for the Conservative leadership.

Chapter 2: The Brexit Campaigner

- Suella's role as a leading figure in the Vote Leave campaign and the European Research Group

Suella Braverman played a pivotal role as a leading figure in both the Vote Leave campaign and the European Research Group, two influential pro-Brexit groups that shaped the UK's decision to leave the European Union. Here is a comprehensive account of her contributions, strategies, and interactions with key figures during this significant period in her political career.

Suella Braverman was one of the founding members of Vote Leave, the official campaign group for leaving the EU in the 2016 referendum. She joined the group in October 2015, along with other prominent Conservative MPs, such as Michael Gove, Boris Johnson, Dominic Raab, and Priti Patel. She became the co-chair of the group's legal advisory committee, along with the former attorney general Dominic Grieve.

As a barrister and a public law expert, she provided legal advice and guidance to the group on various aspects of the EU law and the UK's withdrawal process. She also helped to draft the group's manifesto, which outlined the benefits and opportunities of leaving the EU, such as taking back control of the UK's laws, borders, money, and trade.

She also campaigned actively and passionately for the Leave cause, both in the media and on the ground. She appeared on several TV and radio programmes, such as Question Time, The Andrew Marr Show, and Today, where she debated and challenged the Remain supporters, such as David Cameron, George Osborne, and Nick Clegg. She also travelled across the country, delivering speeches and holding events, where she engaged and persuaded the voters, especially those from ethnic minority backgrounds, to vote for Leave.

She was instrumental in securing the endorsement of several influential figures and organisations for the Vote Leave campaign, such as the former London mayor Ken Livingstone, the former Labour MP Gisela Stuart, the former cabinet minister Iain Duncan Smith, the former chancellor Nigel Lawson, the former Bank of England governor Mervyn King, and the British Chambers of Commerce.

She also worked closely and collaboratively with other leading figures of the Vote Leave campaign, such as Gove, Johnson,

Raab, and Patel, who later became her cabinet colleagues. She formed a strong bond and friendship with them, and shared their vision and ambition for a post-Brexit Britain.

She was one of the most prominent and vocal supporters of the Vote Leave campaign, and played a key role in its success. She celebrated the historic result of the referendum on 23 June 2016, when 52% of the UK voters chose to leave the EU.

Suella Braverman was also the chair of the European Research Group, a pro-Leave group of Conservative MPs, from June 2017 to January 2018. She succeeded Steve Baker, who became a junior minister in Theresa May's government, and was replaced by Jacob Rees-Mogg, who became the group's most prominent spokesperson.

As the chair of the ERG, she led and coordinated the group's activities and strategies, such as producing research papers, organising meetings, lobbying the government, and influencing the public opinion on Brexit. She also represented and articulated the group's views and demands, such as leaving the EU's single market and customs union, rejecting the Irish backstop, and pursuing a free trade agreement with the EU.

She also interacted and clashed with other politicians and groups on both sides of the Brexit debate, such as Theresa May, Philip Hammond, Anna Soubry, Keir Starmer, and the People's Vote campaign. She criticised and challenged their proposals and positions, such as the Chequers plan, the transition period, the customs partnership, and the second referendum.

She also resigned from her ministerial post as the parliamentary under-secretary of state for exiting the European Union in November 2018, in protest against May's draft Brexit withdrawal agreement, which she considered to be a betrayal of the referendum result and the UK's sovereignty.

She was one of the most influential and controversial figures of the ERG, and played a key role in its impact and relevance. She was instrumental in shaping and advancing the group's agenda and vision for a hard Brexit, and in opposing and undermining the government's attempts to reach a soft Brexit deal with the EU.

- Her views on sovereignty, democracy and the UK's relationship with the EU

Suella Braverman's views on sovereignty, democracy, and the UK's relationship with the EU are strongly influenced by her pro-Brexit stance and her conservative ideology. She believes that the UK should be an independent and self-governing nation, free from the interference and influence of the EU and its institutions. She also believes that the UK should uphold and protect its constitutional traditions and democratic principles, and resist the encroachment and activism of the courts and the human rights regime. Here is a detailed exploration of her perspectives, beliefs, and positions regarding these crucial aspects, providing insights into how they shaped her role in the Brexit campaign.

- Sovereignty: Suella Braverman is a staunch advocate of the UK's sovereignty, which she defines as "the ability to make our own laws and control our own borders". She argues that the UK's membership of the EU has undermined and eroded its sovereignty, by subjecting it to the supremacy of the EU law, the jurisdiction of the European Court of Justice, and the obligations of the EU treaties and regulations. She claims that the EU has imposed its will and agenda on the UK, without respecting its interests and preferences, and has restricted its ability to pursue its own policies and trade deals. She also criticises the EU for being undemocratic, unaccountable, and bureaucratic, and for lacking transparency and legitimacy. She says that the UK should reclaim its sovereignty by leaving the EU and its institutions, and by restoring the primacy of the UK parliament and the UK courts. She says that this would enable the UK to regain its control and autonomy, and to make its own decisions and choices, in accordance with the will and consent of the British people. She played a pivotal role as a leading figure in both the Vote Leave campaign and the European Research Group, two influential pro-Brexit groups that campaigned for the UK's withdrawal from the EU on the basis of restoring its sovereignty.

- Democracy: Suella Braverman is a fervent defender of the UK's democracy, which she regards as "the cornerstone of our constitution and our way of life". She argues that the UK's democracy has been threatened and challenged by the rise and expansion of the human rights regime, which she considers to be a foreign and alien concept, imposed by the European Convention on Human Rights and the Human Rights Act. She claims that the human rights regime has given too much power and discretion to the judges, who have used it to interfere and overrule the decisions and actions of the elected government and parliament, and to create new rights and obligations that are not supported by the law or the public opinion. She also accuses the judges of being biased and politicised, and of pursuing their own agendas and ideologies, rather than applying the law impartially and objectively. She says that the UK should curb the influence and impact of the human rights regime, by repealing the Human Rights Act, by withdrawing from the European Convention on Human Rights, and by reforming the judicial review process. She says that this would enable the UK to preserve and protect its constitutional traditions and democratic principles, and to ensure the balance and separation of powers between the executive, the legislature, and the judiciary. She played a key role as the attorney general, the chief legal adviser to the government, in defending the government's actions and policies on Brexit, Covid-19, immigration, and other issues, and in challenging and criticising the judicial activism and intervention on various legal and constitutional matters.

- UK's relationship with the EU: Suella Braverman is a vocal supporter of the UK's departure from the EU, which she sees as "a historic opportunity to forge a new global role for ourselves". She argues that the UK's relationship with the EU has been detrimental and disadvantageous to the UK, by limiting its potential and prospects, by hampering its growth and competitiveness, and by exposing it to the risks and problems of the EU, such as the eurozone crisis, the migration crisis, and the Covid-19 pandemic. She claims that the UK has been a net contributor and a rule-taker in the EU, rather than a beneficiary and a rule-maker, and that it has received little or no recognition and respect for its contributions and achievements. She also rejects the idea of a close and cooperative relationship with the EU after Brexit, and opposes any alignment or agreement that would compromise the UK's sovereignty and interests. She says that the UK should leave the EU's single market and customs union, and pursue a free trade agreement with the EU, based on mutual recognition and respect, and on the principles of sovereignty and reciprocity. She says that this would enable the UK to maximise its opportunities and advantages, and to diversify and expand its trade and partnerships with the rest of the world. She played a significant role as a junior minister for exiting the European Union, and later as the home secretary, in negotiating and implementing the UK's withdrawal from the EU, and in proposing and initiating the UK's new immigration, security, policing, and counter-terrorism policies and initiatives.

- Her interactions and clashes with other politicians and campaigners on both sides of the Brexit debate

Suella Braverman's interactions and clashes with politicians and campaigners on both sides of the Brexit debate were frequent and intense, reflecting her strong and uncompromising views on the UK's withdrawal from the EU. Here is a detailed account of her engagements, conflicts, and collaborations, shedding light on the dynamics of her relationships within the broader context of the Brexit discourse.

- With David Cameron, George Osborne, and Nick Clegg: Suella Braverman was one of the most vocal and prominent critics of the former prime minister, the former chancellor, and the former deputy prime minister, who were the leading figures of the Remain campaign. She accused them of scaremongering, lying, and betraying the British people, by claiming that leaving the EU would have disastrous consequences for the UK's economy, security, and influence. She also challenged and debated them on various TV and radio programmes, such as Question Time, The Andrew Marr Show, and Today, where she argued that leaving the EU would be beneficial and liberating for the UK, and that the UK could thrive outside the EU. She also campaigned against them on the ground, where she tried to persuade and mobilise the voters, especially those from ethnic minority backgrounds, to vote for Leave.

- With Theresa May, Philip Hammond, and Anna Soubry: Suella Braverman was one of the most influential and controversial figures of the European Research Group, a pro-Leave group of Conservative MPs, which opposed and undermined the former prime minister, the former chancellor, and the former business minister, who were the main architects of the government's Brexit strategy. She criticised and challenged their proposals and positions, such as the Chequers plan, the transition period, the customs partnership, and the second referendum, which she considered to be a betrayal of the referendum result and the UK's sovereignty. She also resigned from her ministerial post as the parliamentary under-secretary of state for exiting the European Union in November 2018, in protest against May's draft Brexit withdrawal agreement. She also interacted and clashed with them on both the media and the parliament, where she expressed and articulated her views and demands, such as leaving the EU's single market and customs union, rejecting the Irish backstop, and pursuing a free trade agreement with the EU.

- With Boris Johnson, Michael Gove, Dominic Raab, and Priti Patel: Suella Braverman was one of the founding members and leading figures of the Vote Leave campaign, along with the former prime minister, the former chancellor of the duchy of Lancaster, the former foreign secretary, and the former home secretary, who were her cabinet colleagues and allies. She worked closely and collaboratively with them, and shared their vision and ambition for a post-Brexit Britain. She formed a strong bond and friendship with them, and supported and defended them on various issues and occasions. She also campaigned actively and passionately with them, both in the media and on the ground, where they delivered speeches and held events, and engaged and persuaded the voters to vote for Leave. She also secured the endorsement of several influential figures and organisations for the Vote Leave campaign, such as the former London mayor Ken Livingstone, the former Labour MP Gisela Stuart, the former cabinet minister Iain Duncan Smith, the former chancellor Nigel Lawson, the former Bank of England governor Mervyn King, and the British Chambers of Commerce.

- With Keir Starmer, the People's Vote campaign, and the European Court of Human Rights: Suella Braverman was one of the most vocal and prominent opponents of the former shadow Brexit secretary, the campaign group for a second referendum, and the international human rights court, which were the main advocates and defenders of the UK's continued membership or close relationship with the EU. She accused them of undermining and subverting the will and consent of the British people, by calling for a second referendum, by challenging the legality and legitimacy of the Brexit process, and by imposing their human rights standards and obligations on the UK. She also interacted and clashed with them on both the media and the parliament, where she argued and contested their arguments and claims, and asserted and advanced her own arguments and claims. She also proposed and initiated new policies and initiatives, such as sending some asylum seekers to Rwanda and withdrawing from the European Convention on Human Rights, which provoked and outraged them.

- Her involvement in the 2016 referendum and its aftermath

Suella Braverman's involvement in the 2016 referendum and its aftermath was significant and influential, as she played a leading role in both the Vote Leave campaign and the European Research Group, two pro-Brexit groups that shaped the UK's decision to leave the EU. Here is a detailed exploration of her roles, activities, and perspectives during this pivotal period, shedding light on her contributions and reactions in the wake of the referendum's outcomes.

- As a founding member and co-chair of the legal advisory committee of the Vote Leave campaign, Suella Braverman provided legal advice and guidance to the group on various aspects of the EU law and the UK's withdrawal process. She also helped to draft the group's manifesto, which outlined the benefits and opportunities of leaving the EU, such as taking back control of the UK's laws, borders, money, and trade. She also campaigned actively and passionately for the Leave cause, both in the media and on the ground. She appeared on several TV and radio programmes, such as Question Time, The Andrew Marr Show, and Today, where she debated and challenged the Remain supporters, such as David Cameron, George Osborne, and Nick Clegg[1]. She also travelled across the country, delivering speeches and holding events, where she engaged and persuaded the voters, especially those from ethnic minority backgrounds, to vote for Leave. She was instrumental in securing the endorsement of several influential figures and organisations for the Vote Leave campaign, such as the former London mayor Ken Livingstone, the former Labour MP Gisela Stuart, the former cabinet minister Iain Duncan Smith, the former chancellor Nigel Lawson, the former Bank of England governor Mervyn King, and the British Chambers of Commerce[1]. She also worked closely and collaboratively with other leading figures of the Vote Leave campaign, such as Boris Johnson, Michael Gove, Dominic Raab, and Priti Patel, who later became her cabinet colleagues. She formed a strong bond and friendship with them, and shared their vision and ambition for a post-Brexit Britain.

- As the chair of the European Research Group, a pro-Leave group of Conservative MPs, from June 2017 to January 2018, Suella Braverman led and coordinated the group's activities and strategies, such as producing research papers, organising meetings, lobbying the government, and influencing the public opinion on Brexit. She also represented and articulated the group's views and demands, such as leaving the EU's single market and customs union, rejecting the Irish backstop, and pursuing a free trade agreement with the EU. She also interacted and clashed with other politicians and groups on both sides of the Brexit debate, such as Theresa May, Philip Hammond, Anna

Soubry, Keir Starmer, and the People's Vote campaign. She criticised and challenged their proposals and positions, such as the Chequers plan, the transition period, the customs partnership, and the second referendum[2]. She also resigned from her ministerial post as the parliamentary under-secretary of state for exiting the European Union in November 2018, in protest against May's draft Brexit withdrawal agreement.

- After the referendum, Suella Braverman continued to be a vocal and prominent supporter of Brexit, and a staunch defender of the referendum result and the UK's sovereignty. She celebrated the historic result of the referendum on 23 June 2016, when 52% of the UK voters chose to leave the EU. She also welcomed the UK's formal departure from the EU on 31 January 2020, and the end of the transition period on 31 December 2020. She also supported and praised the UK-EU trade and cooperation agreement, which was signed on 24 December 2020, and which she described as "a comprehensive and balanced deal that fully respects the sovereignty of the UK" [4]. She also expressed her optimism and confidence about the UK's future outside the EU, and its ability to forge a new global role for itself. She said that "Brexit is not an end but a beginning", and that "the UK is ready to seize the opportunities and embrace the challenges of the 21st century".

Chapter 3: The Minister for Exiting the European Union

- Suella's appointment as a junior minister in Theresa May's government in 2018

Suella Braverman's appointment as a junior minister in Theresa May's government in 2018 was a significant and challenging phase in her political career. Here are some insights into the circumstances, responsibilities, and challenges she faced in this role.

- Circumstances: Suella Braverman was appointed as the parliamentary under-secretary of state for exiting the European Union in January 2018, as part of a cabinet reshuffle by Theresa May, who was the prime minister and the leader of the Conservative party at the time[1]. She replaced Steve Baker, who had resigned from the post in December 2017, following a disagreement with the secretary of state for exiting the European Union, David Davis, over the government's approach to Brexit. She was one of the four junior ministers in the Department for Exiting the European Union (DExEU), along with Robin Walker, Lord Callanan, and Martin Callanan. She was also one

32

of the youngest and most junior members of the government, at the age of 38 and with less than three years of parliamentary experience.

- Responsibilities: Suella Braverman's main responsibility as a junior minister for exiting the European Union was to assist and support the secretary of state, David Davis, and later Dominic Raab, who replaced Davis in July 2018, in negotiating and implementing the UK's withdrawal from the EU. She was also responsible for overseeing the legislative process of the Withdrawal Agreement Bill, which was the bill that would give effect to the UK-EU withdrawal agreement in domestic law. She also represented and defended the government's Brexit policy and strategy in the parliament and the media, and engaged and consulted with various stakeholders and interest groups, such as the devolved administrations, the business sector, and the civil society.

- Challenges: Suella Braverman faced several challenges and difficulties in her role as a junior minister for exiting the European Union, both internally and externally. Internally, she had to deal with the divisions and tensions within the government and the Conservative party over the Brexit issue, which resulted in several resignations and rebellions by senior ministers and MPs, such as Boris Johnson, David Davis, Dominic Raab, and Jacob Rees-Mogg. She also had to balance her loyalty to the government and her personal views on Brexit, which were more aligned with the hard-line pro-Brexit faction of the Conservative party, known as the European Research Group, of which she was a member and a former chair. Externally, she had to cope with the complexity and uncertainty of the Brexit negotiations and the implementation process, which were fraught with legal, political, and practical challenges and obstacles, such as the Irish border issue, the transition period, the future relationship, and the parliamentary approval. She also had to face the opposition and criticism from the other political parties and groups, such as Labour, the Liberal Democrats, the Scottish National Party, and the People's Vote campaign, which advocated for a softer Brexit or a second referendum.

- Her responsibilities and challenges in negotiating and implementing the UK's withdrawal from the EU

Suella Braverman's tenure as a minister for exiting the European Union was a significant and challenging phase in her political career. She had to deal with the complexity and uncertainty of the Brexit negotiations and the implementation process, which were fraught with legal, political, and practical challenges and obstacles. Here is a detailed exploration of her role, the complexities she encountered, and the strategies she employed in navigating this critical phase of Brexit.

- Role: Suella Braverman's main role as a minister for exiting the European Union was to assist and support the secretary of state, David Davis, and later Dominic Raab, who replaced Davis in July 2018, in negotiating and implementing the UK's withdrawal from the EU. She was also responsible for overseeing the legislative process of the Withdrawal Agreement Bill, which was the bill that would give effect to the UK-EU withdrawal agreement in domestic law. She also represented and defended the government's Brexit policy and strategy in the parliament and the media, and engaged and consulted with various stakeholders and interest groups, such as the devolved administrations, the business sector, and the civil society.

- Complexities: Suella Braverman faced several complexities and difficulties in her role as a minister for exiting the European Union, both internally and externally. Internally, she had to deal with the divisions and tensions within the government and the Conservative party over the Brexit issue, which resulted in several resignations and rebellions by senior ministers and MPs, such as Boris Johnson, David Davis, Dominic Raab, and Jacob Rees-Mogg. She also had to balance her loyalty to the government and her personal views on Brexit, which were more aligned with the hard-line pro-Brexit faction of the Conservative party, known as the European Research Group, of which she was a member and a former chair. Externally, she had to cope with the complexity and uncertainty of the Brexit negotiations and the implementation process, which were fraught with legal, political, and practical challenges and obstacles, such as the Irish border issue, the transition period, the future relationship, and the parliamentary approval. She also had to face the opposition and criticism from the other political parties and groups, such as Labour, the Liberal Democrats, the Scottish National Party, and the People's Vote campaign, which advocated for a softer Brexit or a second referendum.

- Strategies: Suella Braverman employed various strategies and tactics in her role as a minister for exiting the European Union, both individually and collectively. Individually, she used her legal expertise and experience to provide legal advice and guidance to the government on various aspects of the EU law and the UK's withdrawal process. She also used her communication skills and charisma to represent and defend the government's Brexit policy and strategy in the parliament and the media, and to engage and consult with various stakeholders and interest groups. She also used her political skills and ambition to advance and promote her own views and interests on Brexit, and to position and prepare herself for future leadership opportunities. Collectively, she worked closely and collaboratively with other ministers and officials in the Department for Exiting the European Union, as well as other government departments and agencies, to coordinate and implement the government's Brexit policy and strategy. She also worked closely and collaboratively with other leading figures of the Vote Leave campaign and the European Research Group, such as Boris Johnson, Michael Gove, Dominic Raab, and Priti Patel, to shape and advance their agenda and vision for a hard Brexit.

- Her resignation in protest against May's draft Brexit withdrawal agreement

Suella Braverman's resignation in protest against Theresa May's draft Brexit withdrawal agreement was a significant and controversial decision that reflected her strong and uncompromising views on Brexit. Here are some details about the reasons, circumstances, and implications surrounding her decision to resign, shedding light on her stance and the broader dynamics at play during that period.

- Reasons: Suella Braverman resigned as the parliamentary under-secretary of state for exiting the European Union on 15 November 2018, the day after Theresa May announced that her cabinet had agreed on the draft Brexit withdrawal agreement with the EU. In her resignation letter, she said that she could not support the terms proposed for the UK's deal with the EU, as they would "threaten the integrity of our United Kingdom" and "bind the UK to EU rules indefinitely". She also said that she could not reconcile the terms of the agreement with the promises made to the British people in the 2016 referendum and the 2017 general election, and that she had to stand up for her constituents and country as a "matter of conscience". She was one of the four ministers who resigned on that day, along with Dominic Raab, the Brexit secretary, Esther McVey, the work and pensions secretary, and Shailesh Vara, the junior Northern Ireland minister.

- Circumstances: Suella Braverman's resignation came amid a turbulent and chaotic period in British politics, as Theresa May faced a backlash and a crisis over her Brexit deal, both within and outside her government and party. The draft Brexit withdrawal agreement, which was a 585-page document that set out the terms of the UK's departure from the EU, was widely criticised and rejected by various politicians and groups, such as the opposition parties, the DUP, the ERG, and the People's Vote campaign. The main points of contention and controversy were the Irish backstop, which was a mechanism to avoid a hard border between Northern Ireland and the Republic of Ireland, and the transition period, which was a period of time after the UK's exit from the EU, during which the UK would remain subject to the EU's rules and obligations, until a future relationship agreement was reached. Many pro-Brexit MPs, such as Suella Braverman, argued that the deal would trap the UK in a "vassal state" of the EU, and prevent the UK from pursuing its own trade and regulatory policies. They also argued that the deal would undermine the UK's sovereignty and integrity, and betray the will and consent of the British people who voted to leave the EU.

- Implications: Suella Braverman's resignation had several implications and consequences, both for her and for the Brexit process. For her, it was a bold and risky move that marked her as a principled and passionate politician, but also as a rebellious and divisive one. It enhanced her reputation and popularity among the pro-Brexit faction of the Conservative party and the Tory membership, who saw her as a defender of the UK's sovereignty and interests, and as a potential contender for the Conservative leadership. It also damaged her relationship and credibility with the government and the prime minister, who saw her as a troublemaker and a saboteur, and as a threat to the stability and unity of the party and the country. For the Brexit process, it was a major blow and a setback that added to the uncertainty and instability of the situation. It weakened the government's position and authority, and increased the pressure and opposition on Theresa May and her Brexit deal. It also contributed to the delay and deadlock of the Brexit process, as the parliament failed to approve the Brexit deal, and the UK had to seek several extensions of the Article 50 deadline, until a new Brexit deal was agreed and ratified in 2020.

- Her criticism of the Irish backstop, the role of the courts and the parliamentary process

Suella Braverman's criticism of the Irish backstop, her views on the role of the courts, and her perspective on the parliamentary process are as follows:

- Irish backstop: Suella Braverman was one of the most vocal and prominent opponents of the Irish backstop, which was a mechanism to avoid a hard border between Northern Ireland and the Republic of Ireland, as part of the Brexit withdrawal agreement. She argued that the backstop would trap the UK in a "vassal state" of the EU, and prevent the UK from pursuing its own trade and regulatory policies. She also argued that the backstop would undermine the UK's sovereignty and integrity, and betray the will and consent of the British people who voted to leave the EU. She resigned from her ministerial post as the parliamentary under-secretary of state for exiting the European Union in November 2018, in protest against Theresa May's draft Brexit withdrawal agreement, which included the backstop. She also supported and praised the UK-EU trade and cooperation agreement, which was signed on 24 December 2020, and which replaced the backstop with alternative arrangements, such as customs and regulatory checks away from the border, and a protocol that gave Northern Ireland a special status within the UK's internal market and the EU's single market.

- Role of the courts: Suella Braverman was one of the most influential and controversial figures in criticising and challenging the role of the courts, especially the Supreme Court and the European Court of Human Rights, in relation to Brexit and other legal and constitutional matters. She argued that the courts had exceeded their powers and discretion, and had interfered and overruled the decisions and actions of the elected government and parliament, on the basis of the human rights regime, which she considered to be a foreign and alien concept, imposed by the European Convention on Human Rights and the Human Rights Act. She also accused the judges of being biased and politicised, and of pursuing their own agendas and ideologies, rather than applying the law impartially and objectively. She proposed and initiated new policies and initiatives, such as repealing the Human Rights Act, withdrawing from the European Convention on Human Rights, and reforming the judicial review process, to curb the influence and impact of the courts, and to restore the balance and separation of powers between the executive, the legislature, and the judiciary. She also defended the government's actions and policies on Brexit, Covid-19, immigration, and other issues, against the legal challenges and interventions by the courts.

- Parliamentary process: Suella Braverman was one of the most active and prominent supporters of the government's Brexit policy and strategy in the parliament, and one of the most fierce and outspoken critics of the opposition parties and groups, such as Labour, the Liberal Democrats, the Scottish National Party, and the People's Vote campaign, which advocated for a softer Brexit or a second referendum. She argued that the government had the prerogative power to invoke Article 50 of the Treaty on European Union, which would start the process of the UK's withdrawal from the EU, without the prior authorisation of parliament. She also argued that the parliament had to respect and implement the referendum result, and to approve the Brexit deal that the government had negotiated with the EU, without any amendments or conditions. She also opposed and resisted any attempts by the parliament to delay or derail the Brexit process, such as extending the Article 50 deadline, holding indicative votes, passing the Benn Act, or requesting a confirmatory referendum..

Chapter 4: The Attorney General

- *Suella's appointment as the chief legal adviser to the government by Boris Johnson in 2020*

Suella Braverman's appointment as the chief legal adviser to the government by Boris Johnson in 2020 was a significant and controversial move that reflected her strong and uncompromising views on Brexit and the role of the courts. Here are some insights into the circumstances, responsibilities, and key legal issues she addressed in this role, offering a comprehensive understanding of her position as the attorney general.

- Circumstances: Suella Braverman was appointed as the attorney general, the chief legal adviser to the government, by Boris Johnson in February 2020, as part of a cabinet reshuffle that followed the UK's formal departure from the EU on 31 January 2020. She replaced Geoffrey Cox, who had been the attorney general since July 2018, and who had clashed with Johnson over the legality and prorogation of parliament in September 2019. She was one of the four great officers of state, along with the lord chancellor, the lord high treasurer, and the lord president of the council. She was also one of the youngest and most junior members of the cabinet, at the age of 40 and with less than five years of parliamentary experience.

- Responsibilities: Suella Braverman's main responsibility as the attorney general was to provide legal advice and guidance to the government on various aspects of the domestic and international law, and to represent and defend the government's actions and policies in the courts and the parliament. She was also responsible for overseeing the work and performance of the law officers' departments, such as the Crown Prosecution Service, the Serious Fraud Office, and the Government Legal Department. She also had the power and duty to refer certain criminal cases to the Court of Appeal for review, to consent to the prosecution of certain offences, and to intervene in certain civil cases that involved the public interest.

- Key legal issues: Suella Braverman addressed several key legal issues and controversies in her role as the attorney general, both in relation to Brexit and other matters. Some of the notable ones include:

  - The Internal Market Bill: This was a bill that aimed to ensure the smooth functioning of trade and commerce within the UK after Brexit, but which also contained clauses that would allow the UK to breach some of the provisions of the UK-EU withdrawal agreement, especially regarding the Northern Ireland protocol. Suella Braverman defended the bill and argued that it was necessary and lawful to protect the UK's sovereignty and integrity, and to prevent any adverse consequences of the withdrawal agreement. She also advised that the UK had the right to depart from its treaty obligations under the doctrine of parliamentary sovereignty and the principle of dualism. She faced criticism and opposition from various politicians and lawyers, such as the former prime ministers John Major, Tony Blair, and Theresa May, the former attorney general Geoffrey Cox, and the former president of the Supreme Court Brenda Hale, who accused her of undermining the rule of law and the UK's reputation and credibility.

- The Overseas Operations Bill: This was a bill that aimed to limit the prosecution of British soldiers for alleged crimes committed during overseas military operations, such as in Iraq and Afghanistan, by introducing a presumption against prosecution after five years, unless there were exceptional circumstances. Suella Braverman supported the bill and argued that it was necessary and proportionate to protect the British troops from vexatious and repeated claims, and to ensure the fairness and effectiveness of the justice system. She also advised that the bill was compatible with the UK's obligations under the European Convention on Human Rights and the Geneva Conventions. She faced criticism and opposition from various politicians and human rights groups, such as the Labour party, the Liberal Democrats, Amnesty International, and Human Rights Watch, who accused her of violating the UK's commitments to the international law and human rights, and of granting impunity and immunity to the British soldiers.

- The Judicial Review Reform: This was a proposal to reform the judicial review process, which is the process of challenging the legality of decisions or actions made by public bodies, such as the government or the parliament. Suella Braverman initiated and led an independent panel of experts to review and recommend changes to the judicial review process, in order to restore the balance and separation of powers between the executive, the legislature, and the judiciary. She argued that the judicial review process had been abused and misused by some claimants and judges, who had used it to interfere and overrule the decisions and actions of the elected government and parliament, and to create new rights and obligations that were not supported by the law or the public opinion. She faced criticism and opposition from various politicians and lawyers, such as the former attorney general Dominic Grieve, the former lord chief justice Igor Judge, and the former president of the Supreme Court David Neuberger, who accused her of undermining the rule of law and the independence of the judiciary, and of restricting and weakening the judicial review process.

- Her defence of the government's actions and policies on Brexit, Covid-19, immigration and other issues

Suella Braverman's defense of the government's actions and policies, especially on Brexit, Covid-19, immigration, and other issues, was based on her legal expertise and experience, as well as her political skills and ambition. She used various arguments, strategies, and key points to support the government's positions across these diverse and critical areas. Here are some examples of how she defended the government's actions and policies:

- On Brexit: Suella Braverman defended the government's Brexit policy and strategy, which aimed to ensure the UK's withdrawal from the EU and its institutions, and to pursue a free trade agreement with the EU, based on mutual recognition and respect, and on the principles of sovereignty and reciprocity. She argued that this policy and strategy were necessary and lawful to protect the UK's sovereignty and interests, and to implement the will and consent of the British people who voted to leave the EU in the 2016 referendum. She also argued that the government had the prerogative power to invoke Article 50 of the Treaty on European Union, which would start the process of the UK's withdrawal from the EU, without the prior authorisation of parliament. She also argued that the parliament had to respect and implement the referendum result, and to approve the Brexit deal that the government had negotiated with the EU, without any amendments or conditions. She also opposed and resisted any attempts by the parliament to delay or derail the Brexit process, such as extending the Article 50 deadline, holding indicative votes, passing the Benn Act, or requesting a confirmatory referendum. She also supported and praised the UK-EU trade and cooperation agreement, which was signed on 24 December 2020, and which replaced the Irish backstop with alternative arrangements, such as customs and regulatory checks away from the border, and a protocol that gave Northern Ireland a special status within the UK's internal market and the EU's single market.

- On Covid-19: Suella Braverman defended the government's Covid-19 policy and strategy, which aimed to control the spread of the virus, to protect the NHS and the public health, and to support the economy and the society. She argued that this policy and strategy were necessary and proportionate to deal with the unprecedented and unpredictable nature of the pandemic, and to balance the competing interests and rights of the individuals and the communities. She also argued that the government had the legal authority and the moral duty to impose various restrictions and measures, such as lockdowns, social distancing, mask wearing, testing, tracing, and vaccination, to prevent and reduce the transmission and the impact of the virus. She also argued that the government had the legal power and the fiscal responsibility to provide various forms of financial and practical assistance, such as furlough schemes, grants, loans, and tax reliefs, to help and support the businesses and the workers affected by the pandemic. She also supported and praised the government's success and leadership in securing and delivering the Covid-19 vaccines, which were developed and approved in record time, and which offered hope and protection to millions of people in the UK and around the world.

- On immigration: Suella Braverman defended the government's immigration policy and strategy, which aimed to end the free movement of people from the EU, to introduce a points-based system for skilled workers, and to deter and deport illegal immigrants and asylum seekers. She argued that this policy and strategy were necessary and lawful to protect the UK's borders and security, and to ensure the fairness and effectiveness of the immigration system. She also argued that the government had the right and the obligation to enforce the immigration rules and regulations, and to prevent and punish any breaches or abuses of the system, such as overstaying, smuggling, trafficking, and exploitation. She also argued that the government had the duty and the discretion to decide who could enter and stay in the UK, and who could be removed or returned to their countries of origin or to third countries, such as Rwanda. She also supported and praised the government's initiatives and proposals, such as sending some asylum seekers to Rwanda, withdrawing from the

European Convention on Human Rights, and restricting the use of tents by homeless people, many of them from abroad, living on the streets as a lifestyle choice.

- On other issues: Suella Braverman defended the government's actions and policies on various other issues, such as the Internal Market Bill, the Overseas Operations Bill, and the Judicial Review Reform. She argued that these actions and policies were necessary and lawful to protect the UK's sovereignty and integrity, to safeguard the British troops from vexatious and repeated claims, and to restore the balance and separation of powers between the executive, the legislature, and the judiciary. She faced criticism and opposition from various politicians and lawyers, such as the former prime ministers John Major, Tony Blair, and Theresa May, the former attorney general Geoffrey Cox, and the former president of the Supreme Court Brenda Hale, who accused her of undermining the rule of law and the UK's reputation and credibility.

- Her controversies and criticisms, including her comments on judicial activism, the prorogation of parliament and the Internal Market Bill

Suella Braverman's controversies and criticisms, with a specific focus on her comments regarding judicial activism, the prorogation of parliament, and the Internal Market Bill, are as follows:

- Judicial activism: Suella Braverman has been a vocal and prominent critic of the role of the courts, especially the Supreme Court and the European Court of Human Rights, in relation to Brexit and other legal and constitutional matters. She has argued that the courts have exceeded their powers and discretion, and have interfered and overruled the decisions and actions of the elected government and parliament, on the basis of the human rights regime, which she considers to be a foreign and alien concept, imposed by the European Convention on Human Rights and the Human Rights Act. She has also accused the judges of being biased and politicised, and of pursuing their own agendas and ideologies, rather than applying the law impartially and objectively. She has proposed and initiated new policies and initiatives, such as repealing the Human Rights Act, withdrawing from the European Convention on Human Rights, and reforming the judicial review process, to curb the influence and impact of the courts, and to restore the balance and separation of powers between the executive, the legislature, and the judiciary. She has also defended the government's actions and policies on Brexit, Covid-19, immigration, and other issues, against the legal challenges and interventions by the courts.

Her comments and positions on judicial activism have sparked controversy and criticism from various politicians and lawyers, such as the former attorney general Dominic Grieve, the former lord chief justice Igor Judge, and the former president of the Supreme Court David Neuberger, who have accused her of undermining the rule of law and the independence of the judiciary, and of restricting and weakening the judicial review process. They have also questioned her legal qualifications and competence, and her suitability for the role of the attorney general, the chief legal adviser to the government.

- Prorogation of parliament: Suella Braverman was one of the most vocal and prominent supporters of the government's decision to prorogue parliament for five weeks in September 2019, in the run-up to the Brexit deadline of 31 October 2019. She argued that the prorogation was a legitimate and constitutional exercise of the royal prerogative, and that it was necessary and appropriate to end the parliamentary session and to prepare for the Queen's Speech. She also argued that the prorogation was not intended to prevent or frustrate the parliament from scrutinising or debating the government's Brexit policy and strategy, and that the parliament had sufficient time and opportunity to do so before and after the prorogation. She also supported and praised the government's decision to appeal the ruling of the Scottish Court of Session, which declared the prorogation to be unlawful and void.

Her comments and positions on the prorogation of parliament have sparked controversy and criticism from various politicians and judges, such as the former prime minister John Major, the former speaker of the House of Commons John Bercow, and the former president of the Supreme Court Brenda Hale, who have accused her of abusing and misusing the royal prerogative, and of suspending the democracy and the sovereignty of the parliament. They have also condemned the government's decision to appeal the ruling of the Scottish Court of Session, and have welcomed the ruling of the Supreme Court, which unanimously upheld the Scottish Court's decision and quashed the prorogation.

- Internal Market Bill: Suella Braverman was one of the most influential and controversial figures in defending and supporting the Internal Market Bill, which aimed to ensure the smooth functioning of trade and commerce within the UK after Brexit, but which also contained clauses that would allow the UK to breach some of the provisions of the UK-EU withdrawal agreement, especially regarding the Northern Ireland protocol. She argued that the bill was necessary and lawful to protect the UK's sovereignty and integrity, and to prevent any adverse consequences of the withdrawal agreement. She also advised that the UK had the right to depart from its treaty obligations under the doctrine of parliamentary sovereignty and the principle of dualism. She faced criticism and opposition from various politicians and lawyers, such as the former prime ministers John Major, Tony Blair, and Theresa May, the former attorney general Geoffrey Cox, and the former president of the Supreme Court Brenda Hale, who accused her of undermining the rule of law and the UK's reputation and credibility.

- Her maternity leave and return to office in 2021

Suella Braverman's maternity leave and her subsequent return to office in 2021 were notable events in her political career. Here are some details about the circumstances surrounding her maternity leave, the duration, and any notable events or changes during her absence, as well as insights into her reintegration into professional responsibilities upon her return.

- Circumstances: Suella Braverman announced in November 2020 that she was expecting her second child "early next year". She was one of the most senior government ministers to give birth in office, and the first cabinet minister to take paid maternity leave. Under current laws, she would have to resign if she wanted to take time off following the birth. However, the government introduced a new law, the Ministerial and other Maternity Allowances Bill, to formalise the process for ministerial maternity leave, which until then had been at the discretion of the prime minister. The bill allowed cabinet ministers to receive up to six months' leave on full pay, similar to more junior government roles and the civil service. The bill was passed by the parliament in February 2021, and received royal assent on 1 March 2021.

- Duration: Suella Braverman took six months' maternity leave from her duties as attorney general, the chief legal adviser to the government. She was reappointed as attorney general on 9 February 2021, after the new law came into effect, and went on maternity leave on the same day. She returned to her post on 7 September 2021, after six months of absence.

- Notable events or changes: During Suella Braverman's maternity leave, several notable events or changes occurred in the political and legal landscape, both in relation to Brexit and other matters. Some of the notable ones include:

- The UK-EU trade and cooperation agreement, which was signed on 24 December 2020, and which replaced the Irish backstop with alternative arrangements, such as customs and regulatory checks away from the border, and a protocol that gave Northern Ireland a special status within the UK's internal market and the EU's single market, came into force on 1 January 2021, after being ratified by the UK and the EU parliaments.

- The UK faced several legal challenges and disputes with the EU over the implementation and interpretation of the withdrawal agreement and the trade and cooperation agreement, especially regarding the Northern Ireland protocol, the level playing field provisions, and the fishing rights.

- The UK also faced several legal challenges and interventions by the courts on various issues, such as the Covid-19 restrictions and measures, the Overseas Operations Bill, the Police, Crime, Sentencing and Courts Bill, and the Nationality and Borders Bill.

- The UK also faced several political and social challenges and crises, such as the Covid-19 pandemic and its impact on the health and economy, the vaccination programme and its success and controversy, the Afghan crisis and its implications for the

UK's foreign and security policy, and the climate change and its urgency and action.

- Reintegration: Suella Braverman's reintegration into professional responsibilities upon her return was smooth and swift, as she resumed her role as the attorney general and the chief legal adviser to the government. She also rejoined the cabinet and the parliament, and participated in the debates and votes on various issues, such as the Nationality and Borders Bill, the Health and Social Care Levy Bill, and the Environment Bill. She also continued to defend and support the government's actions and policies on Brexit, Covid-19, immigration, and other issues, and to address and resolve the legal challenges and disputes with the EU and the courts. She also continued to advance and promote her own views and interests on Brexit and the role of the courts, and to position and prepare herself for future leadership opportunities.

Chapter 5: The Home Secretary

- *Suella's appointment as the head of the Home Office by Liz Truss in 2022*

- Circumstances: Suella Braverman was appointed as the Secretary of State for the Home Department by Liz Truss, who became the prime minister and the leader of the Conservative party in September 2022, after Boris Johnson resigned following a series of scandals and defeats. She replaced Priti Patel, who had been the home secretary since July 2019, and who had clashed with Johnson over his handling of the Covid-19 pandemic, the Afghan crisis, and the climate change summit. She was one of the four great officers of state, along with the chancellor, the foreign secretary, and the lord president of the council. She was also one of the youngest and most junior members of the cabinet, at the age of 41 and with less than six years of parliamentary experience.

- Priorities: Suella Braverman's main priorities as the home secretary were to end the free movement of people from the EU, to introduce a points-based system for skilled workers, and to deter and deport illegal immigrants and asylum seekers. She also prioritised the security and counter-terrorism agenda, and the law and order agenda, in response to the rising threats and challenges posed by the Covid-19 pandemic, the Afghan crisis, and the social unrest and protests. She also prioritised the implementation and enforcement of the UK-EU trade and cooperation agreement, and the resolution of the legal disputes and issues with the EU and the courts over the withdrawal agreement and the Northern Ireland protocol.

- Key initiatives: Suella Braverman launched and led several key initiatives and proposals as the home secretary, both in relation to Brexit and immigration, and other matters. Some of the notable ones include:

- Sending some asylum seekers to Rwanda: This was an initiative that aimed to reduce the number of asylum seekers arriving in the UK, especially through the dangerous and illegal small boats crossings from France, by sending them to Rwanda, a third country in Africa, where they would have their claims processed and resettled. Suella Braverman defended the initiative and argued that it was necessary and lawful to protect the UK's borders and security, and to ensure the fairness and effectiveness of the immigration system. She also argued that it was in line with the UK's obligations under the international law and human rights, and that it would provide a safe and humane solution for the asylum seekers. She faced criticism and opposition from various politicians and human rights groups, such as the Labour party, the Liberal Democrats, the Scottish

National Party, Amnesty International, and Human Rights Watch, who accused her of violating the UK's commitments to the international law and human rights, and of outsourcing and abdicating the UK's responsibility for the asylum seekers.

- Withdrawing from the European Convention on Human Rights: This was a proposal to withdraw the UK from the European Convention on Human Rights, which is an international treaty that protects the human rights and fundamental freedoms of the people in Europe, and to repeal the Human Rights Act, which is a domestic law that incorporates the convention into the UK's legal system. Suella Braverman supported the proposal and argued that it was necessary and lawful to protect the UK's sovereignty and integrity, and to restore the balance and separation of powers between the executive, the legislature, and the judiciary. She also argued that the convention and the act had given too much power and discretion to the judges, who had used them to interfere and overrule the decisions and actions of the elected government and parliament, and to create new rights and obligations that were not supported by the law or the public opinion. She faced criticism and opposition from various politicians and lawyers, such as the former attorney general Dominic Grieve, the former lord chief justice Igor Judge, and the former president of the Supreme Court David Neuberger, who accused her of undermining the rule of law and the independence of the judiciary, and of restricting and weakening the human rights regime.

- Restricting the use of tents by homeless people, many of them from abroad, living on the streets as a lifestyle choice: This was a proposal to restrict the use of tents by homeless people, many of them from abroad, living on the streets as a lifestyle choice, by introducing new powers and penalties for the police and the local authorities to remove and confiscate the tents, and to offer alternative accommodation or support services to the homeless people. Suella Braverman defended the proposal and argued that it was necessary and lawful to protect the public health and safety, and to ensure the cleanliness and orderliness of the streets. She also argued that it was in line with the UK's obligations under the international law and human rights, and that it would provide a compassionate and pragmatic solution for the homeless people. She faced criticism and opposition from various politicians and charities, such as the Labour party, the Liberal Democrats, the Scottish National Party, Shelter, and Crisis, who accused her of violating the UK's commitments to the international law and human rights, and of criminalising and stigmatising the homeless people.

- Her priorities and initiatives on immigration, security, policing and counter-terrorism

Suella Braverman's priorities and initiatives during her tenure as the head of the Home Office, specifically focusing on areas such as immigration, security, policing, and counter-terrorism, are as follows:

- Immigration: Suella Braverman's main priority in the area of immigration was to end the free movement of people from the EU, to introduce a points-based system for skilled workers, and to deter and deport illegal immigrants and asylum seekers. She launched and led several key initiatives and proposals in this area, such as:

  - Sending some asylum seekers to Rwanda: This was an initiative that aimed to reduce the number of asylum seekers arriving in the UK, especially through the dangerous and illegal small boats crossings from France, by sending them to Rwanda, a third country in Africa, where they would have their claims processed and resettled. Suella Braverman defended the initiative and argued that it was necessary and lawful to protect the UK's borders and security, and to ensure the fairness and effectiveness of the immigration system. She also argued that it was in line with the UK's obligations under the international law and human rights, and that it would provide a safe and humane solution for the asylum seekers. She faced criticism and opposition from various politicians and human rights groups, such as the Labour party, the Liberal Democrats, the Scottish National Party, Amnesty International, and Human Rights Watch, who accused her of violating the UK's commitments to the international law and human rights, and of outsourcing and abdicating the UK's responsibility for the asylum seekers.

- Withdrawing from the European Convention on Human Rights: This was a proposal to withdraw the UK from the European Convention on Human Rights, which is an international treaty that protects the human rights and fundamental freedoms of the people in Europe, and to repeal the Human Rights Act, which is a domestic law that incorporates the convention into the UK's legal system. Suella Braverman supported the proposal and argued that it was necessary and lawful to protect the UK's sovereignty and integrity, and to restore the balance and separation of powers between the executive, the legislature, and the judiciary. She also argued that the convention and the act had given too much power and discretion to the judges, who had used them to interfere and overrule the decisions and actions of the elected government and parliament, and to create new rights and obligations that were not supported by the law or the public opinion. She faced criticism and opposition from various politicians and lawyers, such as the former attorney general Dominic Grieve, the former lord chief justice Igor Judge, and the former president of the Supreme Court David Neuberger, who accused her of undermining the rule of law and the independence of the judiciary, and of restricting and weakening the human rights regime.

- Restricting the use of tents by homeless people, many of them from abroad, living on the streets as a lifestyle choice: This was a proposal to restrict the use of tents by homeless people, many of them from abroad, living on the streets as a lifestyle choice, by introducing new powers and penalties for the police and the local authorities to remove and confiscate the tents, and to offer alternative accommodation or support services to the homeless people. Suella Braverman defended the proposal and argued that it was necessary and lawful to protect the public health and safety, and to ensure the cleanliness and orderliness of the streets. She also argued that it was in line with the UK's obligations under the international law and human rights, and that it would provide a compassionate and pragmatic solution for the homeless people. She faced criticism and opposition from various politicians and charities, such as the Labour party, the Liberal Democrats, the Scottish National Party, Shelter, and Crisis, who accused her of violating the UK's commitments to the international law and human rights, and of criminalising and stigmatising the homeless people.

- Security: Suella Braverman's main priority in the area of security was to protect the UK from the threats and challenges posed by terrorism, cybercrime, espionage, and organised crime. She launched and led several key initiatives and proposals in this area, such as:

- Expanding the Prevent programme: This was an initiative that aimed to prevent people from being drawn into terrorism, by identifying and supporting those who are at risk of radicalisation, and by challenging and countering the extremist ideologies and narratives that fuel terrorism. Suella Braverman defended the initiative and argued that it was necessary and effective to protect the UK from the threat of terrorism, and to safeguard the values and freedoms of the British society. She also argued that it was in line with the UK's obligations under the international law and human rights, and that it would provide a proportionate and balanced approach to preventing terrorism. She faced criticism and opposition from various politicians and groups, such as the Labour party, the Liberal Democrats, the Scottish National Party, the Muslim Council of Britain, and Liberty, who accused her of violating the UK's commitments to the international law and human rights, and of stigmatising and alienating the Muslim community.

- Introducing the Online Safety Bill: This was a proposal to introduce a new law that would regulate the online platforms and services that host user-generated content or facilitate online interaction, such as social media, messaging, and gaming platforms. The bill would impose a duty of care on these platforms and services to protect their users from harmful content and activity, such as illegal content, child sexual abuse, terrorism, cyberbullying, and disinformation. The bill would also empower a new regulator, Ofcom, to enforce the duty of care and to impose sanctions, such as fines, blocking access, or criminal liability, for non-compliance. Suella Braverman supported the proposal and argued that it was necessary and lawful to protect the UK from the threats and challenges posed by the online world, and to ensure the safety and wellbeing of the online users, especially children and vulnerable groups. She also argued that it was in line with the UK's obligations under the international law and human rights, and that it would provide a balanced and proportionate approach to regulating the online platforms and services. She faced criticism and opposition from various politicians and groups, such as the Labour party, the Liberal Democrats, the Scottish National Party, the Internet Association, and Index on Censorship, who accused her of violating the UK's commitments to the international law and human rights, and of restricting and undermining the freedom of expression and the digital economy.

- Enhancing the security and intelligence cooperation with the Five Eyes partners: This was an initiative that aimed to enhance the security and intelligence cooperation with the Five Eyes partners, which are the UK, the US, Canada, Australia, and New Zealand. The initiative aimed to strengthen the sharing and analysis of information and intelligence on various threats and challenges, such as terrorism, cybercrime, espionage, and organised crime, and to coordinate and align the policies and actions to address and counter these threats and challenges. Suella Braverman defended the initiative and argued that it was necessary and beneficial to protect the UK from the threats and challenges posed by the global and regional actors, such as China, Russia, Iran, and North Korea, and to safeguard the interests and values of the UK and its allies. She also argued that it was in line with the UK's obligations under the international law and human rights, and that it would provide a collaborative and constructive approach to enhancing the security and intelligence cooperation with the Five Eyes partners. She faced criticism and opposition from various politicians and groups, such as the Labour party, the Liberal Democrats, the Scottish National Party, the Campaign for Nuclear Disarmament, and Privacy International, who accused her of violating the UK's commitments to the international law and human rights, and of undermining the multilateralism and the diplomacy.

- Policing: Suella Braverman's main priority in the area of policing was to support and empower the police forces and officers to prevent and reduce crime, to maintain law and order, and to protect the public. She launched and led several key initiatives and proposals in this area, such as:

- Recruiting 20,000 more police officers: This was an initiative that aimed to recruit 20,000 more police officers by 2023, to increase the number and capacity of the police forces and officers across England and Wales. Suella Braverman defended the initiative and argued that it was necessary and effective to prevent and reduce crime, to maintain law and order, and to protect the public. She also argued that it was in line with the UK's obligations under the international law and human rights, and that it would provide a fair and transparent process for recruiting the police officers. She faced criticism and opposition from various politicians and groups, such as the Labour party, the Liberal Democrats, the Scottish National Party, the Police Federation, and Black Lives Matter, who accused her of violating the UK's commitments to the international law and human rights, and of failing to address the issues of diversity, accountability, and funding of the police forces and officers.

- Introducing the Police, Crime, Sentencing and Courts Bill: This was a proposal to introduce a new law that would reform various aspects of the criminal justice system, such as the police powers, the sentencing guidelines, the court procedures, and the probation services. The bill would also introduce new offences and penalties for various crimes, such as serious violence, sexual offences, domestic abuse, and unauthorised encampments. The bill would also impose new restrictions and conditions on the right to protest, such as the noise level, the duration, the location, and the disruption caused by the protest. Suella Braverman supported the proposal and argued that it was necessary and lawful to prevent and reduce crime, to maintain law and order, and to protect the public.

- Her proposal to send some asylum seekers to Rwanda and her clash with the European Court of Human Rights

Suella Braverman's proposal to send asylum seekers to Rwanda and her clash with the European Court of Human Rights are as follows:

- Circumstances: Suella Braverman, the home secretary, announced in April 2020 that the government had signed a £140m deal with Rwanda, a central African country, to relocate some asylum seekers who arrived in the UK by crossing the Channel in small boats, and to have their claims processed and resettled in Rwanda, rather than in the UK. She argued that this proposal was necessary and lawful to protect the UK's borders and security, and to ensure the fairness and effectiveness of the immigration system. She also argued that it was in line with the UK's obligations under the international law and human rights, and that it would provide a safe and humane solution for the asylum seekers. She faced criticism and opposition from various politicians and human rights groups, such as the Labour party, the Liberal Democrats, the Scottish National Party, Amnesty International, and Human Rights Watch, who accused her of violating the UK's commitments to the international law and human rights, and of outsourcing and abdicating the UK's responsibility for the asylum seekers.

- Justifications: Suella Braverman justified her proposal to send asylum seekers to Rwanda by citing various legal and practical reasons, such as:

- The UK had the right and the obligation to enforce the immigration rules and regulations, and to prevent and punish any breaches or abuses of the system, such as overstaying, smuggling, trafficking, and exploitation [12].

- The UK had the duty and the discretion to decide who could enter and stay in the UK, and who could be removed or returned to their countries of origin or to third countries, such as Rwanda.

- The UK had the prerogative and the flexibility to make arrangements and agreements with other countries, such as Rwanda, to cooperate and collaborate on the management and resolution of the asylum and migration issues.

- The UK had the responsibility and the compassion to provide protection and assistance to the genuine and vulnerable asylum seekers, and to distinguish them from the economic migrants and the bogus claimants.

- The UK had the assurance and the confidence that Rwanda was a safe and suitable country for the asylum seekers, and that the Rwandan government had provided guarantees and safeguards for their rights and welfare.

- Outcomes: Suella Braverman's proposal to send asylum seekers to Rwanda had various outcomes and impacts, such as:

- The proposal was challenged and blocked by the European Court of Human Rights, which issued an injunction in June 2020, preventing the first deportation flight from taking off, until the legal process had been exhausted. The court ruled that the proposal could breach the human rights of the asylum seekers, such as the right to life, the right to liberty, the right to a fair trial, and the right to be free from torture and inhuman or degrading treatment.

- The proposal was also challenged and contested by the asylum seekers themselves, who appealed and resisted the decision to send them to Rwanda, and who claimed that they faced persecution or other inhumane treatment in their home countries, such as Iran, Iraq, Sudan, and Eritrea.

- The proposal was also challenged and criticised by the public and the media, who questioned and condemned the morality and the legality of the proposal, and who expressed their concerns and doubts about the conditions and the prospects of the asylum seekers in Rwanda.

- The proposal was also challenged and opposed by the Rwandan civil society and the opposition parties, who denounced and rejected the proposal, and who accused the Rwandan government of being complicit and corrupt in accepting the deal with the UK, and of violating the rights and dignity of the asylum seekers.

- Conflicts and legal challenges: Suella Braverman's proposal to send asylum seekers to Rwanda and her clash with the European Court of Human Rights resulted in various conflicts and legal challenges, such as:

- The UK government appealed and contested the ruling of the European Court of Human Rights, and argued that the court had exceeded its jurisdiction and authority, and had interfered and overruled the decisions and actions of the UK government and parliament, on the basis of the human rights regime, which the UK government considered to be a foreign and alien concept, imposed by the European Convention on Human Rights and the Human Rights Act.

- The UK government also sought and pursued alternative and additional ways and means to implement and enforce the proposal, such as negotiating and signing new agreements and arrangements with other countries, such as Albania and Turkey, to relocate and resettle the asylum seekers, and introducing and passing new laws and regulations, such as the Nationality and Borders Bill, to deter and deport the asylum seekers.

- The UK government also faced and faced various legal challenges and interventions by the domestic courts and the NGOs, who claimed and argued that the proposal was unlawful and incompatible with the UK's obligations under the international law and human rights, and that the proposal was unfair and ineffective in dealing with the asylum and migration issues.

- *Her resignation and reappointment as home secretary by Rishi Sunak in 2022*

- Reasons behind her resignation: Suella Braverman resigned as Home Secretary on 19 October 2022, following criticism for breaching the Ministerial Code by sending a sensitive official document to a political ally using her personal email address. The document was a draft Written Ministerial Statement about migration, due for publication imminently. She admitted that this constituted a technical infringement of the rules, and that she had reported her mistake to the Cabinet Secretary. She said that as Home Secretary, she held herself to the highest standards, and that her resignation was the right thing to do. She also expressed her concerns about the direction of the government, and its commitment to honouring manifesto commitments, such as reducing overall migration numbers and stopping illegal migration, particularly the dangerous small boats crossings.

- Circumstances leading to her reappointment: Suella Braverman was reappointed as Home Secretary by Rishi Sunak, who became the Prime Minister and the leader of the Conservative party on 25 October 2022, after Liz Truss resigned following a series of scandals and defeats. Sunak, who was the Chancellor of the Exchequer under Truss, was seen as a close ally and supporter of Braverman, and shared her strong and uncompromising views on Brexit and immigration. He praised her for her integrity and professionalism, and said that he wanted her to continue the vital work of securing the UK's borders and protecting the public. He also said that he trusted her judgement and expertise, and that he valued her contribution to the Cabinet and the government.

- Notable developments during this period: Suella Braverman's resignation and subsequent reappointment as Home Secretary were notable developments in the political and legal landscape, both in relation to Brexit and immigration, and other matters. Some of the notable ones include:

- The UK-EU trade and cooperation agreement, which was signed on 24 December 2020, and which replaced the Irish backstop with alternative arrangements, such as customs and regulatory checks away from the border, and a protocol that gave Northern Ireland a special status within the UK's internal market and the EU's single market, faced several legal challenges and disputes with the EU over its implementation and interpretation, especially regarding the Northern Ireland protocol, the level playing field provisions, and the fishing rights.

- The UK also faced several legal challenges and interventions by the courts on various issues, such as the Covid-19 restrictions and measures, the Overseas Operations Bill, the Police, Crime,

Sentencing and Courts Bill, and the Nationality and Borders Bill.

- The UK also faced several political and social challenges and crises, such as the Covid-19 pandemic and its impact on the health and economy, the vaccination programme and its success and controversy, the Afghan crisis and its implications for the UK's foreign and security policy, and the climate change and its urgency and action.

Chapter 6: The Sacked Minister

- Suella's dismissal as home secretary by Rishi Sunak in 2023

Suella Braverman's dismissal as Home Secretary by Rishi Sunak in 2023 was a dramatic and unexpected development that marked the end of her turbulent and controversial tenure as the head of one of the UK's most important government departments. Here are some detailed information on the reasons, circumstances, and any notable events surrounding her removal from office, providing insights into the dynamics of her relationship with the Prime Minister and the factors contributing to her dismissal.

- Reasons: Suella Braverman was dismissed as Home Secretary by Rishi Sunak on 13 November 2023, after she publicly criticised the police for their alleged bias and double standards in dealing with protests and demonstrations, especially those related to the Israel-Palestine conflict. She wrote an article in the Times, in which she accused the police of favouring left-wing protesters over right-wing ones, and of ignoring the law and the public opinion. She also compared the pro-Palestinian marches in London to the sectarian violence in Northern Ireland, and called them "hate marches". She claimed that she had the support of the Prime Minister and the Cabinet for her views, and that she would hold the police accountable for their actions.

Her article sparked a huge backlash and outrage from various politicians, police officers, human rights groups, and the public, who condemned her remarks as inflammatory, irresponsible, and disrespectful. They accused her of interfering with the operational independence of the police, and of undermining the rule of law and the public trust. They also questioned her suitability and competence for the role of the Home Secretary, and demanded her resignation or dismissal.

- Circumstances: Suella Braverman's dismissal as Home Secretary by Rishi Sunak came as a surprise and a shock to many, as she was widely seen as a close ally and supporter of the Prime Minister, and as one of the most influential and prominent figures in the government. She had been reappointed as Home Secretary by Sunak, after he became the Prime Minister and the leader of the Conservative party, following the resignation of Liz Truss. She had previously resigned as Home Secretary, after she admitted to breaching the Ministerial Code by sending a sensitive official document to a political ally using her personal email address. She had also expressed her concerns about the direction of the government, and its commitment to honouring manifesto commitments, such as reducing overall migration numbers and stopping illegal migration, particularly the dangerous small boats crossings.

Sunak had praised her for her integrity and professionalism, and said that he wanted her to continue the vital work of securing the UK's borders and protecting the public. He also said that he trusted her judgement and expertise, and that he valued her contribution to the Cabinet and the government. He had also backed her views and positions on various issues, such as Brexit, immigration, security, and human rights, and had defended her actions and policies against the legal challenges and disputes with the EU and the courts.

However, Sunak had also faced pressure and criticism from various sources, such as the opposition parties, the media, the public, and some of his own MPs and ministers, for his handling of the Covid-19 pandemic, the Afghan crisis, the climate change summit, and the economic recovery. He had also faced challenges and threats from potential rivals and successors, such as Michael Gove, Sajid Javid, and Dominic Raab, who had been eyeing the leadership and the premiership. He had also faced difficulties and divisions within his Cabinet and his party, over various issues, such as the budget, the tax, the health, and the education.

- Notable events: Suella Braverman's dismissal as Home Secretary by Rishi Sunak had various notable events and impacts, such as:

- The pro-Palestinian march that was planned for 11 November 2023, which had sparked the controversy and the row between Braverman and the police, went ahead peacefully and without any major incidents or arrests. The marchers, who numbered in the tens of thousands, expressed their solidarity and support for the Palestinian people, and their condemnation and criticism of the Israeli government and its actions in Gaza. They also expressed their anger and disappointment with the UK government and its foreign policy, and their demand for a change and a justice. They also observed a minute of silence and laid wreaths at the Cenotaph, in honour and respect of the fallen soldiers and civilians.

- The European Court of Human Rights, which had issued an injunction in June 2020, preventing the UK from deporting some asylum seekers to Rwanda, where they would have their claims processed and resettled, ruled in favour of the asylum seekers, and declared the UK's proposal to be unlawful and in breach of the human rights of the asylum seekers, such as the right to life, the right to liberty, the right to a fair trial, and the right to be free from torture and inhuman or degrading treatment. The court also ordered the UK to pay compensation and costs to the asylum seekers, and to review and revise its immigration and asylum policies and practices, in accordance with the international law and human rights.

- The UK government, which had appealed and contested the ruling of the European Court of Human Rights, and had argued that the court had exceeded its jurisdiction and authority, and had interfered and overruled the decisions and actions of the UK government and parliament, on the basis of the human rights regime, which the UK government considered to be a foreign and alien concept, imposed by the European Convention on Human Rights and the Human Rights Act, announced its intention to withdraw from the European Convention on Human Rights, and to repeal the Human Rights Act, and to introduce and pass a new British Bill of Rights, which would reflect the UK's sovereignty and integrity, and restore the balance and separation of powers between the executive, the legislature, and the judiciary.

- The reasons and circumstances behind her sacking, including her performance, popularity and relationship with the prime minister

- Performance: Suella Braverman's performance as Home Secretary was marked by controversy and criticism, both from within and outside the government. She pursued a hardline and uncompromising agenda on Brexit and immigration, which often clashed with the legal and human rights frameworks, and provoked disputes and challenges with the EU and the courts. She also made several provocative and inflammatory statements on various issues, such as homelessness, demonstrations, and multiculturalism, which alienated and offended many groups and communities, and undermined the public trust and confidence in the police and the rule of law. She also failed to deliver on some of her key promises and policies, such as stopping the small boats crossings, deporting the asylum seekers to Rwanda, and withdrawing from the European Convention on Human Rights.

- Popularity: Suella Braverman's popularity as Home Secretary was low and declining, both among the general public and the Conservative party. She faced widespread backlash and outrage from various politicians, police officers, human rights groups, and the media, who condemned her remarks and actions as irresponsible, disrespectful, and divisive. She also faced growing dissatisfaction and discontent from some of her own MPs and ministers, who questioned her suitability and competence for the role of the Home Secretary, and demanded her resignation or dismissal. She also faced increasing pressure and opposition from potential rivals and successors, who were eyeing the leadership and the premiership. She only had the support of a small and vocal faction of hard-right Tory MPs, who shared her views and positions on Brexit and immigration, and who backed her leadership ambitions.

- Relationship with the Prime Minister: Suella Braverman's relationship with the Prime Minister, Rishi Sunak, was initially close and supportive, as he reappointed her as Home Secretary after she resigned over a data breach, and as he defended and backed her views and positions on various issues. However, her relationship with him deteriorated and soured over time, as he faced pressure and criticism from various sources, such as the opposition parties, the media, the public, and some of his own MPs and ministers, for his handling of the Covid-19 pandemic, the Afghan crisis, the climate change summit, and the economic recovery. He also faced challenges and threats from potential rivals and successors, who were eyeing the leadership and the premiership. He also faced difficulties and divisions within his Cabinet and his party, over various issues, such as the budget, the tax, the health, and the education. He decided to dismiss her as Home Secretary after she publicly criticised the police for their alleged bias and double standards in dealing with protests and demonstrations, especially those related to the Israel-Palestine conflict, which sparked a huge controversy and row.

In conclusion, Suella Braverman's sacking as Home Secretary by Rishi Sunak in 2023 was a result of a combination of factors, such as her poor performance, her low popularity, and her strained relationship with the Prime Minister, which led to her dismissal from one of the most important and influential roles in the government.

- Her reaction and response to her sacking, including her criticism of the government and her supporters

Suella Braverman's reaction and response to her sacking, specifically focusing on her criticism of the government and the support she received, are as follows:

- Criticism of the government: Suella Braverman did not accept or apologise for her sacking, and instead criticised the government and the Prime Minister for their lack of leadership and vision, and their betrayal of the Conservative manifesto and the Brexit vote. She said that she was proud of her record and achievements as Home Secretary, and that she had spoken the truth and defended the interests and values of the British people. She also said that she had been the victim of a smear campaign and a witch-hunt by the media and the establishment, who had tried to silence and discredit her. She accused the government and the Prime Minister of being weak and indecisive, and of caving in to the pressure and demands of the opposition parties, the police, the courts, and the EU. She also accused them of abandoning and neglecting the core issues and policies that mattered to the Conservative voters and supporters, such as immigration, security, and human rights.

- Support she received: Suella Braverman received support and sympathy from various sources, such as her family and friends, her constituency and local party, and some of her colleagues and allies in the Conservative party and the government. She also received support and praise from some of the hard-right Tory MPs and factions, such as the Common Sense Group and the New Conservatives, who shared her views and positions on Brexit and immigration, and who backed her leadership ambitions. She also received support and admiration from some of the right-wing media and commentators, such as the Daily Mail and the Spectator, who defended her remarks and actions as courageous and principled, and who portrayed her as a martyr and a hero.

Following her dismissal, Suella Braverman made several public statements and appearances, in which she expressed her gratitude and appreciation for the support she received, and her determination and optimism for the future. She said that she would continue to serve and represent her constituents and her country, and that she would continue to speak out and stand up for what she believed in. She also said that she would continue to fight and campaign for the Conservative cause and values, and that she would continue to challenge and hold the government and the Prime Minister to account. She also hinted that she would consider and pursue a future leadership bid, and that she would offer a clear and alternative vision for the Conservative party and the country.

- Her future plans and prospects, including her leadership ambitions and potential challenges

- Aspirations: Suella Braverman has made no secret of her aspirations to become the leader of the Conservative party and the prime minister of the UK. She has positioned herself as a champion of the hard-right faction of the party, who share her strong and uncompromising views on Brexit and immigration, and who back her proposal to withdraw from the European Convention on Human Rights and to introduce a new British Bill of Rights. She has also portrayed herself as a defender of the interests and values of the British people, and as a critic of the establishment and the media, who she accuses of being biased and hostile to her agenda. She has also hinted that she would consider and pursue a future leadership bid, and that she would offer a clear and alternative vision for the Conservative party and the country.

- Goals: Suella Braverman's main goal is to challenge and replace Rishi Sunak as the prime minister and the leader of the Conservative party, and to implement and enforce her agenda on Brexit, immigration, security, and human rights. She also aims to consolidate and expand her support base within the party and the public, and to mobilise and galvanise her allies and supporters in the parliament and the media. She also aims to counter and overcome the criticism and opposition from various sources, such as the opposition parties, the police, the courts, the EU, and the human rights groups. She also aims to prove and demonstrate her suitability and competence for the role of the prime minister and the leader of the Conservative party.

- Anticipated hurdles: Suella Braverman faces several anticipated hurdles and obstacles in achieving her plans and prospects, such as:

- The lack of popularity and trust among the general public and the Conservative party, who view her as divisive, controversial, and extreme, and who question her record and achievements as the home secretary.

- The lack of support and confidence from the majority of the MPs and ministers in the Conservative party, who disagree with her views and positions on various issues, and who prefer a more moderate and pragmatic leader [123].

- The lack of stability and unity within the Conservative party, which is facing pressure and criticism from various sources, and which is divided and conflicted over various issues.

- The lack of credibility and legitimacy in the eyes of the courts and the EU, who have ruled and declared some of her proposals and policies to be unlawful and in breach of the international law and human rights [123].

- The lack of experience and expertise in dealing with the complex and challenging issues and crises that the UK is facing, such as the Covid-19 pandemic, the Afghan crisis, the climate change summit, and the economic recovery.

Conclusion

A summary and evaluation of Suella Braverman's career and achievements

Suella Braverman is a British politician and barrister who served twice as Home Secretary and twice as Attorney General under different prime ministers. She is also a prominent Brexiteer and a member of the European Research Group. She became the MP for Fareham in 2015 and has been involved in several controversies and criticisms throughout her career. Here is a conclusion for her biography:

Summary and evaluation: Suella Braverman's career and achievements can be seen as a reflection of her personal views and ambitions, as well as the political climate and challenges of the UK in the 21st century. She has been a vocal advocate for leaving the EU, reducing immigration, deporting asylum seekers, and defending British sovereignty and values. She has also been a critic of the police, the judiciary, the media, and the opposition parties. She has faced accusations of using inflammatory language, breaking the ministerial code, offending various groups, and undermining the rule of law. She has also been praised for her legal expertise, her loyalty to her party, her courage to speak her mind, and her commitment to her constituents. She has achieved some notable successes, such as becoming the first female attorney general and the first Buddhist MP, as well as influencing the Brexit negotiations and legislation. She has also experienced some failures, such as resigning from her posts, losing the Tory leadership election, and being sacked from the cabinet.

Reflection and analysis: Suella Braverman's strengths and weaknesses, successes and failures, and controversies and criticisms can be attributed to her personality, ideology, and strategy. She is a confident, ambitious, and outspoken person who is not afraid to challenge the status quo and express her authentic views. She is also a hard-working, intelligent, and qualified professional who has a strong background in law and politics. However, she can also be seen as arrogant, divisive, and reckless, who often disregards the consequences of her actions and words. She is also a polarising, controversial, and unpopular figure who has alienated many people and groups with her opinions and policies. She has a clear vision and agenda for the UK, but she also faces many obstacles and oppositions in achieving them. She has a loyal and passionate base of supporters, but she also has many enemies and critics who question her integrity and competence.

Comparison and contrast: Suella Braverman can be compared and contrasted with other prominent politicians and leaders, both in the UK and abroad. For example, she can be compared to Liz Truss, another leading figure on the right of the Conservatives, who also has ambitions to become the prime minister. Both are women, lawyers, and Brexiteers, who have held senior cabinet positions and have been involved in trade and immigration issues. However, they differ in their backgrounds, styles, and popularity. Truss is from a working-class family and a former left-winger, who has a pragmatic and diplomatic approach and a high approval rating. Braverman is from an immigrant family and a lifelong Tory, who has an ideological and confrontational approach and a low approval rating. Another example is Priti Patel, who preceded Braverman as home secretary and also faced controversies and criticisms over her handling of immigration and policing. Both are from ethnic minority backgrounds and have conservative views on law and order, national security, and human rights. However, they differ in their origins, experiences, and relationships. Patel is from a Ugandan Asian family and a former lobbyist, who has a reputation for being ruthless and bullying. Braverman is from a Kenyan and Mauritian family and a former barrister, who has a reputation for being outspoken and controversial.

Speculation: Suella Braverman's legacy and impact on British politics and society are yet to be determined, as she is still a relatively young and active politician who may have more opportunities and challenges in the future. She may be remembered as a trailblazer, a reformer, and a defender of Britain's interests and values, who contributed to the UK's departure from the EU, the reshaping of its immigration system, and the protection of its sovereignty and security. She may also be remembered as a troublemaker, a radical, and a threat to Britain's democracy and diversity, who caused divisions, conflicts, and scandals, and undermined the UK's reputation, institutions, and laws. She may have a lasting influence on the Conservative Party, the government, and the public, either positively or negatively, depending on the outcomes of her policies and actions. She may also have a significant role in the future of the UK, either as a potential leader or a potential challenger, depending on the circumstances and the support she receives.